AF314017

BARBARIAN PRAYER

BARBARIAN PRAYER

SELECTED POEMS OF

Sándor Csoóri

Selection by Mátyás Domokos

Foreword by Len Roberts

CORVINA

Acknowledgements
Some of the translations published in this volume
have appeared in *Modern Hungarian Poetry*
(Corvina, Budapest);
The Hungarian P.E.N. bulletin;
The New Hungarian Quarterly; The New York Times;
Sulfur (Eastern Michigan University, Ypsilanti);
and in two volumes of Csoóri's selected poems:
Memory of Snow
(Penmaen Press, Great Barrington)
and *Wings of Knives and Nails*
(Vox Humana, Toronto),
to whose publishers acknowledgement is made.

© Sándor Csoóri, 1989

Translated from the Hungarian
by
Tony Connor, Alan Dixon, Clayton Eshleman,
Andrew Feldmar, Gerard Gorman, I. L. Halasz de Beky,
Daniel Hoffman, Nicholas Kolumban, J. D. McClatchy,
Kenneth McRobbie, Edwin Morgan, Len Roberts,
William Jay Smith, George Szirtes,
with the help of Győző Ferencz,
Gyula Kodolányi, Mária Kőrösy,
Anita Sényi, László Vértes

Edited by Mária Kőrösy

CONTENTS

FOREWORD

SÁNDOR CSOÓRI: WITNESS

Sándor Csoóri's poetry serves as a passionate mirror of post-World War II Hungary. It presents a world of toppled bridges, razed villages, the wounded and the dead, for above all, Csoóri is a witness, an unrelenting witness, to the turmoil of his homeland in recent times. Yet this witness keeps searching for answers, sometimes in the face of a beautiful woman, sometimes in an attachment to nature, and sometimes in the doggedly persistent belief in the value of the search itself. But he does not find answers usually, and most of his poems end with the speaker alone, remembering a past that had once held meaning, considering a future which, at best, will be filled with struggle. The present, under Csoóri's unrelentingly honest perspective, is one of lies and hypocrisy, a time in which the speaker is barely able to maintain his own integrity.

Yet that is one of the major strengths of Sándor Csoóri's poetry: there *is* an individual self who is able to exist, albeit with extreme hardships, in an age and society which values the depersonalization of man. Csoóri's speaker is always an identifiable person, one with a past (however horrific), a present (however despondent), and a future (however tenuous); this is the voice of a human being, presumably the poet himself, who is struggling to maintain his independent individuality. As Csoóri has said: "From the first there has been present in my work, in whichever genre, a general sense of unease. About how to maintain the existence of the human personality in the world amid the great campaigns of depersonalization." ("Autobiographical Note", *ARION* 12 Budapest, 1980.) Csoóri has refused to surrender this concept of selfhood, either to the "great campaigns of depersonalization" or to the abstractions of much contemporary poetry.

The voice of alienation and solitude comes from so deep within him that it is undeniable. When he writes of his own life, whether it be about an early love, or about a time when he idled in the streets of Poland, or about the time when his generation was "good and obedient", there is no doubt in the reader's mind that the speaker has been there, that he has been true to Walt Whitman's words: "I was the man, I suffer'd, I was there". There also is no doubt that this man speaks for his countrymen and not just for himself, and that accounts, justifiably, for his great following in Hungary. Although many of his poems are very grim, indeed, nightmarish, Csoóri's poetry, in its best moments, is redeeming, for it represents man's spirit coming to terms with the hardships of his existence.

Whether due to his temperament, or to his times, or to both, Sándor Csoóri is a master of the elegy; indeed, his most powerful poems are about loss, poems in which the perishability of man is evoked so strongly that the reader often feels as though he is being smothered. In this world of transience Csoóri carves out small, illuminated moments in which the one who is mourned may shine. It is this lyrical intensity, this insistence upon certain moments as inviolable, which show most truly Csoóri's optimistic strain: in the midst of darkness, a loved one's face appears, and that moment must not be lost. These elegiac poems are simple and complex at the same time, for they deal with mythic death as it occurs in everyday existence. Again, he serves as witness and recorder to the lives (and deaths) of his friends and loved ones, as well as to his age.

Sándor Csoóri is also a master of the image, the sensual element which is consistently present in his poetry. His poems are about everyday experiences and thus he fills them with details from our common lives. The presence of these images give the poems their own lives, so to speak, for the poem becomes the world and the world becomes the poem. And Csoóri *does* love the world, no matter how harshly he criticizes it—espresso, a woman's fringed skirt, even the nightmarish image of a twisted automobile, they all show his love of, and commitment to, the world in which we all live. No wonder, then, that his poems remain in the reader's mind, for Csoóri creates a reality in which the reader may situate himself, a reality in which he may also come to see, to witness.

Lastly, and most importantly, both for the social and

poetical valuation of his work, Sándor Csoóri is, without
any doubt, the most prominent artistic spokesman for the
Hungarian people of his time. He has captured the hard-
ships and struggles, as well as the accompanying sense of
loss and guilt, of his generation. Without sacrificing his
poetry to propaganda, he has been able, by absorbing the
social and political turmoil of his period into himself, to
digest these turmoils and re-create them on a personal,
artistic level which is completely authentic. His are the
masterful words of a man who was there, the words of a
daring witness.

May, 1989   *Len Roberts*

MY MOTHER'S A BLACK ROSE

My mother has a headache,
　she won't drink black coffee—
my mother has a headache,
　she doesn't take medicine;
　paler and more silent now
she goes to milk the heifer
　paler and more silent now
　she sweeps and brings washing in.

My mother has visitors,
　men rudely accost her,
my mother is terrified
　her head's in a fluster,
　she tugs at her dark headscarf
she tugs at her loneliness,
　such men should not come again
　frightening her, pitiless.

My mother takes to the highway,
　she doesn't get anywhere
her brow's scarred with poverty
　it burns like a star on her;
　even the lilac flower
bends down and burdens her,
　it weighs on her shoulder,
　its scent is a curse on her.

It's summer on earth, in the air,
　music and harmony,
on the sands of her silence
　she perishes quietly.
　Machines and their produce sing
their magic, their dizziness,
　not one runs to her to say:
command me, I'm yours mistress.

My mother has a headache,
    the void is what weighs her down.
My mother's a black rose,
    she can't put the rainbow on,
    One night she collapses,
she's broken and very small—
    A bird swoops with open beak
    and whisks her off, head and all.

(*George Szirtes*)

REMEMBERING AN OLD STREET

Little crooked street:
Discarded melon slice.
Black seeds are your cobbles,
You are covered with flies.

Your synagogue's face:
A stuffed heifer's face.

The earlocks of your small Jews are curly,
Their skinny hands flat noodles roll,
They only have their god, no department store,
They came riding the winds from Bethlehem.

Who has seen Moses with beard of oakum?
He comes by here every night;
He draws water from the stones,
He draws water from the walls,
And by dawn your pavement is a muddy sight.

My listlessness looks at you,
My pondering eyes glance back from here;
A little Jewish girl returns my greeting,
Her eyes are six-pointed stars of constant fear.

A straw flies up now, caught in air—
You! The living! Can you see?
The little Jewish girl's yellow bone
Flies into a yellow nullity.

It flies to mother: green gas in space,
It flies to father: lampshade on the moon,
It flies to brother: rectangular dry soap
In a shop window of the next world of hope.

Little street, little street, Europe's
Tiny poppy-seed street; death's footprint
Can you see in your black mud,
Despite your eyesight, weakening?

I am moving out, away from you, forever;
Leaving only my memories:
Your windmill trees will grind them up with ease,
And your birds will devour them.

(*Andrew Feldmar*)

GOLDEN PHEASANTS FLYING

Here they were all running, running past my heart:
the late March wind, my father's horse with his head like a burning coal
here my friends ran by with feet dampened in dew,
ran with the great joy of the earth.

The golden pheasants flying through the forest's gate,
a wounded moon driven by the heavens' breathing,
and in showers born of the rending of the clouds
the world was as beautiful as in a future Gospel.

Faces of foliage, of people, faces of waters and of girls,
you never left me forsaken in the happy chase.
We stepped over the sibylline immobility of stones
as across the forgotten dead.

And sea, once only have I seen you, but I've tasted you—
You were the summer's wine, the cooled draught of the universe,
o mystical wing which upraised me from within
above all dry sobriety and my own death.

Where are you, sea, and you, my schoolmates hiding beneath the bridge?
Where are you, ploughs of dawn with which I harrowed the sun?
Wind threading the needle's eye of Spring, revolution of the lilacs,
whose side have you joined up with, now that you've deserted me?

I stand above my village; behind me, the ancient ruin.
The woods are desolate, forlorn the meadows of boyhood.
The golden pheasant scurries among the trees, the wind is scudding too,
and I have no other joy but that I may cry out to them.

(Daniel Hoffman)

I STOLE YOUR FACE

If you should turn from me, you will not be a stranger—
behind you stands the ancient blazon of the sun;
behind you, my life, an immortal shadow, silent
as a totem bird exiled in the golden heaven.

You can hide anew each minute, or reappear;
I shall not search for you behind the snowfall
or in the smarting wilderness of smoky offices
where your phone, a pearly rattler, waits upon its coil.

I am content that once, like heaven's fire, I stole your face
and gave it to other women to make them fair;
content that in my matted body, in my dreams
like a buried statue or legend burnt in tile, you are always there.

(Daniel Hoffman)

BARBARIAN PRAYER

Wrinkled, unrelaxing stone,
rock of mother-daylight, take
me back again into your womb.
Being born was the first error;
the world was what I wanted to be:
lion and tree-root in one,
loving animal and laughing snow,
consciousness of the wind, of heights
pouring their dark ink-blot down—
and here I am cloud-foundered man,
king of a solitary way,
being of a cindery star,
and what I join within myself
splits me at once, because it goes
quickly and only sharpens yearning...
Wrinkled, unrelaxing stone,
rock of mother-daylight, I
stand at the entrance to your womb.

(Edwin Morgan)

SO IT SHOULD NOT BE DARK

The bold bridges and the trees'
impersonal row on the concrete banks
can still be seen;
the afternoon's falling snow on the faces of children running home
can still be seen.

But soot slowly covers the water
and the body's night is falling too.

I think of those who may be destroyed,
who are not shielded by a dream.
Silence whistles into their room like a bullet,
and loneliness like the news of death.

I think of those who may be destroyed,
the Earth is full of them;
no armies protect them, no rose arbors, no scented shirts,
not money's silver fences,
not love.

And in vain they die, for in vain they were born.

I think of those who may be destroyed,
only a hand would be needed, so they should have a homeland,
only another body, so it should not be dark.

(Len Roberts and László Vértes)

AGUE

What is this extraordinary crowding,
this seagull-torrent,
woman's screaming,
ocean-howling?
Trees collapse together
like men hit by sunstroke.
A moment ago I had a grape in my lips,
now I suck sea-ooze.
On my hand hare's blood,
frog-spawn,
silk of a night-gown are drying.
In a green coach of leaves, summer and my skull go driving.
Rain rouses me,
water stills me,
war in prospect hones the body—
Come on, I'll give even brave mouths my boot
if they hold me with their stupidity.
What is this, what is this rage, ague, change?
Poems go pounding through me like freight-trains.
Dispersed—my bones,
my vertebrae,
my brain.
My hand droops like a shot soldier
in trenches of alien beds—
Joyless fingers are busy about me,
with a blue sky they bandage me,
in the gauze of rivers they bind me,
and they carry me prone on the wind,
but where to, where?

(Edwin Morgan)

MY WINTER KINGDOM

I cannot run on ten paths,
I cannot die ten deaths,
well, then, I'll wait for that special one
which sinks me to the depths.

Winter, my kingdom,
is a snowflake kingdom only,
my departing on a hundred paths
is a lone departure only.

(Len Roberts and László Vértes)

FOR ENCOURAGEMENT

Just like the mole whose eyes are the same dark earth
    it crawls through,
just like the wind screaming through the holes in the moon,
    through this pigeon-cave in the world's last cliff,
just like the bullet when it stumbles into a body,
    falling through its own scarred face,
just like the missile when it stabs silently through
    the sky's contractions,
just like the lovers who live up their lives
    and leave nothing for death
    but their coats and umbrellas,
jut like the pilot, a prisoner to the lack of limits,
    who flies higher only to fall
    in fatal love with the earth,
just like the one who always speaks of stones,
    although he doesn't believe in anything
    but the dirt man digs his life from,
on his face love betrays itself, like a tattooed number,
    faded, and still disappearing.

(J. D. McClatchy and Gyula Kodolányi)

I WOULD RATHER RUN BACK

What a crazy saint I am,
eating insects, spending nights
among the roots,
from your weeping
and your body fleeing
into bare rooms, to deserts of rejected eyes,
and stones crawl over me like lice,
and the caterpillar-night, and familiar ants,
I journey companioned by trees
to pay my respect to the snow because it is white,
to lovers because they are in love,
but everywhere the evenings are the same,
the silences the same.
I shun the cities, they yap from the distance
like dogs,
and shun the forests because they are plundered by owls.

I would rather run back to your hair,
to your mouth,
to your creaking wardrobes,
and because you are always craving
I would feed you with myself, my illumination,
my madness, here you are, here is summer,
the blossom of acacia,
blue plum of the seas: the earth,
and I would love you
and I would love you.

(Alan Dixon)

THE STRANGER

Somebody comes and knocks, seeking accommodation,
but can only grin robot-like at the doorhandle,
at the yellow-blossoming room-antennae.
If you don't mind, I mumble, someone's just died,
we want to spend the night in peace and quiet
and talk to him beside some bread, beside some wine,
be part of the forest sounds he used to hear.
Nodding, he's still a stranger in the midst of loss,
though he, too, is born of Earth.

(Kenneth McRobbie and Mária Körösy)

DRY STORM

Still only the roofs
have collapsed in on themselves,
still only the backs of leaves
flutter up like fish.
Last week's papers pump down the road
like accordions
fingered by war invalids.

Now it is only the city's slow smog
that begs around the knees —
but from beyond sight already it quivers
and speeds like light
from a darkening sun.

Not rain,
not hail,
not yet a storm.
Its lightning pricks the skin just above
the heart, warning like a simple lust,
like the stealth of a wind on railway platforms,
the unsteady rhythms of thunder.

It drinks from the Danube,
from your wounds,
it shivers you against the shoulders of strange women,
this is the time for you to leave,
this is the time for you to die,
this is the time for you to rise again,
this is the time for you to escape the stink of gateways:

a deathday
here
can be bought in any shop —
perhaps the fatigued arrival helps,
perhaps the suffering along the lips:
so you came here? good, you may undress now,
rip down the sarcophagus of summer,
shake out the dead's light dust,
I will close the window down on you,
I will close the house down on you,
I will close this day down on you.

(J. D. McClatchy and Gyula Kodolányi)

CANTATA PROFANA
IN MEMORY OF BÉLA BARTÓK

We did not go home today either,
we did not go home, boys.
In vain mother scoured the knives,
in vain she scrubbed
the knotty table.
In the slop of its blood
with its neck slit,
in vain the goose wailed.

We did not send a word,
we did not write a line—
as though a flood had swept away our hands.
Easter is no longer Easter,
the swept house
no longer our house.

*

Who is that old man over there?
Sitting in front of the white wall's ghostly aura,
sitting in the cigarette smoke of the world's end.

His face is a crushed wicker basket.

He might be waiting for us,
looking for us,
wishing to see us,
in the street beyond the window,
in his short-sighted life.

Don't look for us,
don't wait,
you, old man reeking of tobacco,
you, poor, kennel-breasted one.
We are no longer your sons.
If the door opens, it's like a jacknife.

And if we speak,
we rave, like false witnesses.

We would only rush upon you, like a blast,
we would throb beside you
like an old generator.
Plates and wine glasses
would crack,
and our shoulder-length hair—the roots of the continents—
would weave through your stomach,
and you would become a hair-basket,
a hair-man,
a corpse which can be singed.*

(Len Roberts and Anita Sényi)

* This reference to singeing may allude to the practice
of burning the bristles off a pig after it is slaughtered.

ON THE THIRD DAY IT BEGAN TO SNOW

The first day was good
  for forgetting everything;
the second, for remembering everything.
And on the third day it began to snow,
    and the idea was born
    that from now on it would always snow,
    from your forehead to your mouth,
    from your mouth to your lap,
    all along the length of your body,
    all through my life.
The ceiling will snow, the telephone,
    when I pick it up,
the fading childhood sky, when I look back.
Even between thwarted trees and thwarted haystacks,
    the spirit of the snow wanders,
    settling on blacked-out fields,
    crowning the refugees of war.
And I knew then that I would not be alone,
that this snowfall would accompany me wherever I went,
sitting by me on the train,
crossing the sea with me,
in the night of smouldering car-tyres
    and airless towns,
    speaking to me in my mother-tongue
    and conquering countries for me,
    because to conquer countries
    was what you wanted.
And when I no longer have a country, for I won't
    have the strength to confess to it,
    I'll lock myself into this snowfall
    like someone putting on a white shirt,
    a white shirt on the last day.

(Gerard Gorman and Mária Kőrösy)

THE OTHER

I can touch her,
I can kill her,
I can welcome her in,
I can knot myself in her hair
and fly round the earth,
I can pulse inside her,
but she doesn't hear what I say,
my words drown in her blood,
she stands behind her wall of daggers
aiming her face at me
like a desperate message,
then she denies,
evades,
floats off on a cloud
with a memory that is not my flesh,
a shadow I have never worn,
she falls
through my eyes
back into herself,
from her body
back into her body.

(Tony Connor and Mária Kőrösy)

WHITE, WHITENESS

Who looks after you white, whiteness?
Snailshell colour, church, sty colour,
Easter-wall colour? Who mourns for you,
mourning colour, you prodigal-son-white?
Under spider-legs enamel peels off,
the kicked lime scabs,
pilgrim flies spread filth on the lamb-white
pages. Who sighs after you? Who
laments? Who lures you from
the dark chambers of night,
bone colour, sacrifice colour, burning
animals' white of the eye, blight,
childhood, snow-night, snow-day, Eden-sheet
restlessness, only meadow of speechlessness,
white, whiteness?

(Tony Connor and Mária Kőrösy)

CONDITIONAL

I'd like to sit with you
in a room and listen to you,
behind drawn blinds I'd like to sit with you.
Night coming on outside,
inside exposed old beams,
no witnesses
except the solitary fly
(our familiar skating champion)
moving rapidly across the light-globe.
Your exposed thighs would loll
one upon the other like basking seals,
and there'd be music:—
foliage fugues,
mosquito motets,
and scratchy dance-tunes from the sea's worn record.

Through the keyhole we'd observe distant fires—
Vietnam, of course!
Burning villages
going up like fat-soaked paper,
bamboo roofs collapsing
all on a summer's night,
a child's charred face
all on a summer's night,
rags and dragging feet at the world's end
where the lean kine jump over—
acrobats on the wall of death.
All on a summer's night
reassured by strawberries and beer
and the hibernating bear-dream of our eyes
glued to the television...
geometry of expectations.
What else might come
before your body,

before falling asleep,
from the vast space that worms its way
between the close I
and the distant you?

(*Tony Connor and Mária Körösy*)

PROPHECY ABOUT YOUR TIME

It will come,
you'll see, it will come,
before you begin to decay it will come,
the roughcast walls will feel the new morning down in their roots,
new summer,
a long day full of curtained groins and loins,
and water will soak through your canvas shirt,
your bones too will soak in water,
    swimming ahead,
      backward and upward,
as if you were rifling
the crypt of the sea—

it will come,
you'll see, it will come,
before you begin to decay it will come,
a pigeon will bleed as it swoops
and scrapes its belly on stones,
and the sky will be orange with the glow of conductor-wires,
and on heated boulevards
the cars,
    the words,
      the cries will fly about
like pieces of lead shot, like caravans of lead,
and you will walk among them,
under cover
of smoke and of dust,
the invitation of death in the swaying of your body
but nobody will wound you then
because you've no memory,
and nobody will wound you then,
because you no longer live in your wounds—
Insanity! insanity! the mouths will hiss at you
like spouts in a gutter,
and under the sprinklers under their whiskers of water

so will the barnacled pavement—
Insanity! insanity! professional mannequins
with thousands of years of sickly-sweet smiles will flood you
and window-displays will show ants,
ants on the pavement in its grey basin,
ants on the barrack-squares of eyes left wide open,
ants in the clocks, in their beaten up works,
        coming
                and going,
                        and seething,
they'll lay ceremonial
        wreaths of cogwheels
        on emptiness,
it'll be beautiful,
        I tell you, quite beautiful,
because only you can succeed in their place,
who knew how to wait
after the first pain for the succeeding pain,
to hide from red in the black
        and out of the black,
to find a daily embodiment,
to break out in sweat,
        to divide, to persist.

            (*George Szirtes*)

WINGS OF KNIVES AND NAILS

From here to there,
from under his hand into your arm,
from under his hair into your hair,
passenger of floating cherry-stone nowhere never.

Out of mud into the chilly blue,
up, up over the skyscraper of grasses
into the wind,
lodger of fleeting orphanage nowhere never.

The sand, the music, the yellow fever of clay
makes me tremble: I am what they are:
Compassionate body, a time—
exhausting play and yet nowhere and never.

Wings of knives and nails. Cinder
of oracle under my skin.
Always something. Always something.
And yet nowhere and never.

(I. L. Halasz de Beky)

MAY-PROPELLER IS THE HAND

Would it not have been good
to the waist in sunshine,
to the waist in grass,
lying back in the bed of turbulent water?
good on the streets
when many people walk?

Paradise caterpillars in the garden,
adam and eve-shadows—
would it not have been good without the smouldering swamps of blood,
sinless and with impunity
peering out from behind the billets,
like someone who lives for a long time
and could dally for a long time?

and to be white
and black
and green
and superfluous in the armpit-scented herds—

May-propeller is the hand—

Would it not have been good to ascend,
disperse,
raining back to the earth,
good, to open like a sluice,
like a spring-blocking stone to burst,
and good in the bluishness to wait,
good, to think of what I was waiting for,
on time's Monday you,
on time's Tuesday also you,
on time's Wednesday also you.

(I. L. Halasz de Beky)

THE VISITOR'S MEMORIES

I left a piece of my head in that smoky-smelling house, there, right there on the milk-burnt plain of the oven-top, with the bread crust tossed to the dog.

I arrived, uninvited, early in the morning. At first, the waking children merely stared at me from behind the fortifications of their bunched-up quilts: who might I be? what might I want? in what shop did I steal my camomile-yellow shoes? But when I discovered, one by one, their bud-like noses and geranium ears, and before their very eyes did a hairy bear-fist waddle, "grr-grr-grr, my skin is bitten by fleas, the fleas are biting my knees," I saw the little bishops of laughter consecrated by merriment. Their tiny bead-like teeth exploded through the room like popcorn. From the blackened table to the stool, from stool to earthen floor, down to the sandals tossed under the beds. More! More! Don't take the bear away once you have brought him here (their timid mouths would have said had they expressed themselves).

Out of one eye their mother watched the theater tumbling out of no-where. Instead of cat-flaying excitement, or bear-flaying blood adventure, she noticed marching clouds reined in by the serenity in the children's dilated eyes. She continued sitting on her hatchet-hewed milking-stool, drinking her eternal cup of tea. I knew that the sun sets in her liver, that the years support her ramshackle heart with a wooden beam. I also knew that with her blackening dried-plum face, I would appear beneath frosty chandeliers at drink-nursing diplomatic feasts where, wrapped in lettuce, her prematurely-harvested breasts would also be served.

I will arrive at such dinners perhaps by plane, perhaps with iron-plated wings attached to my shoulders, perhaps on the back of a leaf drifting in through an open window, I, the spy for the poor, who is blessed with de-stroyer eyes and who sees everything. My ironed shirt will be the skin of those who have been sophisticatedly flayed, my Golgothically ticking clock their pounding temples, after those of my father, my mother, and this sister as well, sitting before me, the orphan of a familiar but vanishing story, harboring no impassioned revenge, in tea steam breathing through her children's mouths and surviving through her children's flesh the tribute exacted from her womb.

(Clayton Eshleman and Gyula Kodolányi)

MY BEAST

A little beast is visiting me;
she comes, wearing her toes neatly shod.
As she crosses the bridge, I can hear her.
Crows spin above oak trees
like the tires of a hearse.
(Margit Island is being stripped bare.)
The newspaper says we may have snow, much snow.
I think I see snowflakes
in my room.
My beast is coming closer, all in bloom,
like someone who's followed by music—
the drum solo of a waning summer afternoon.

I once saw black girls coming like this in Havana:
they ate oranges on the barricades
(sandbags and red dahlias cluttered the street).
Their sweet gestures were like a demonstration
in the name of a threatened world.

If old billy goat Anacreon
could see what heaven passes over him
at the wind-blown feet of the bridge,
he'd be annoyed.
What flagrant clicking of heels,
protesting death!
The sound of the gentle rubbing of thighs.
The scratching of black sedges.

(Nicholas Kolumban)

THE DOOR CREAKED THRICE

You arrive. Everything in its place:
keys, needles, masks, gloves,
hunchbacked beetles and invading ants, too,
across the kitchen floor.
And down to the cellar and up to the touched Moon
the same drugged ways.
Your home?
   Your country?
      Your open wound?
The door creaked thrice,
when you entered,
thrice did the mirror mist over,
when your thudding arm sank into the table-top;
yet still the eyes which sailed around the earth
look for closing eyelids,
a dream in which there would be room for your body.

Reject this arrival,
this joyless order,
the crimes of the servile feet—
outside deluge-eyed women throng before your house
with the sweetness of catastrophies.

(Gerard Gorman and Mária Kőrösy)

WHISPERS, FOR TWO VOICES

I was there,
yes, I was there,
a voice whispered to me between
two faded chairs: don't go away, do you hear? don't go away!
if you go it will be as if three of you were going!
as if five of you were going,
as if a hundred of you were going,
and in the glass-splintered winter
the trees will wait in vain
for your caresses,
the wheezing thrushes for your crumbs,
do you hear? you could still become the ringmaster of the earth,
the earth's best man—
I was there,
yes, I was there,
I even remember the pulse of the body,
the half-open door, the exposed
nerves
dangling over the threshold—
                        and then the other voice
from behind the murky wardrobe: what are you waiting for?
you will be given
nothing in exchange for quiescence,
fidelity's hibernating heart will always be surrounded by snow,
the nipples of women
could still harden under your fingers,
lips to your lips they could still
pump spring into you, but they return
to their mirrors too quickly,
to the site of their desperation,
and you, messianic buffoon: victim of their boiling blood,

will have to beg for a country
to go with the wounds of your body
while you are still able to stand,
the white shirt a wounded man's bandage.

(*Alan Dixon*)

INSIDE TIME

The days go by faster than I can live.
There's no time to love the crackling leaves,
the poplars that climb the sky,
the pigeons who stand about on the roof.
Dawn abducted me from dawn.
I smell the aroma of my country's past
in the freshly ground coffee.
Honey collects in the hives.
I'm expected here.
I come with the snow-covered wreaths
behind the bird coffins.
More time! Give us more time.
Your voices swoop down
on me, Othello, who's jealous of death.
I get a grip on myself.
I want to write books full of slow rain,
forests full of lechery.
I want to stroll
from bridge to bridge,
wearing blue, yellow and burgundy,
to lure the nude women of postcards
away from their indolent lovers
and idle inside time
like one who gazes at his reflection.

(Nicholas Kolumban)

THE FIRST MOMENTS OF RESURRECTION

The dog sat there on the manure pile,
covered with wounds and chaff of straw.
Enveloped by the stinking smell of Gehenna
sat the dog. The Easter bells pealed
for his wounds—ding-dong, ding-dong.
Wasps crawled out of the walls
of murdered buildings.
Nobody believed
that we had been resurrected!

The light-fingered survivors began
to undress the last dead of the war:
off came the helmets, the boots, the thick socks.
Off the pea jackets.
It looked as if mothers were peeling
grimy clothes off their drunken sons.
My God! What hapened to you,
you hoodlum, you pig, my love!
Look at your sprung Adam's apple.
Your sweet head is bloody!

A southern breeze grazed me;
my fingertips bloomed in the barnyard of death.
I saw the unconquerable hen—
who lived only for the corn.
She struggled, as if possessed,
with the untied shoelaces of the dead.
She pulled and tugged, pecking in the mixture
of mud, hair and empty cartridge.
She all but soared, drunk with good fortune:
having collared the longest spring worm
in the world!

(Nicholas Kolumban)

I'LL GO, I'M GOING

I'll go, I'm going, I'm on my way—
Between one long wait and another, rain stops then starts again,
and trains turn green like ancient copper farthings.
Will it be evening? summer? January?
The hills are left behind, the poplars go,
the bronze dog that has rusted in the scrapyard—
and if by then I've finished reading the poems and papers for the journey
I'll imagine your long hair where wild geese fly,
stray pieces of clothing you might have thrown off behind bushes
and I won't even know whether I love you or not,
for the taste of your mouth and your skin will be there in my mouth,
the taste of unripened peaches, your body in my body,
and every one of the hands with which you once embraced me.

(George Szirtes)

A LATE DEMONSTRATION
IN A FRENCH MINING TOWN

The wind blows, all day the wind blows.
The sparrows of St. Etienne are shivering.
This shiver accompanies me.
You dragged me here, Lord of roads and snow.
I eat a cold orange in front of the Magistrate's palace.
I eat with the ancient mouth
of Zola's poor.
This is a late demonstration.
It feels good to think
that I'm the indisputable hand
in the quiver
of a blue and red neon butterfly.
I'm mouth's greed,
memory that's shattered by a club.
The adult city's head.
I hear police bullets
drop out of the long dead.
From under the cobblestones
I hear the trot of the miners' horses,
blinded.

I appear with all my pasts
in the long, bright streets.
With all my poverty, hymns.
My face becomes shabby like a sack
in front of a shop window, full of furs.
My face grows old in the light of new fires
that are for sale.

(Nicholas Kolumban)

TAR SEAL

Christmas has gone, New Year has gone,
gone are those long wanton days
between Twelfth Night and Candlemas.
Feeble snowfalls put me in a blue funk.
All I did was sit and wait for the arrival of a poem, but my knees
like slag heaps kept crumbling down.
In the evening sometimes I put on a record of the gale
and listened to the howling of the poplars, the leaf-cries,
and came close to howling myself:
leave me alone, let me be, happy wind, truer than I,
you make an iron pail wobble around, whining through the air above my
                 heart,
and I don't want it, don't want it.
But as if someone had put a tar seal to my mouth,
I just sat there, numb.

(William Jay Smith)

MEMORY OF SNOW

Winter sometimes changes its mind
and snow begins to fall
desperately, in thick flakes, as if winter
were afraid it might not last the night.
Best thing to do at such times is to disconnect the phone,
the doorbell, mull some wine on the stove,
pore over old letters,
and go back over your whole life also
as if it had never happened.
As if no gun barrel, no wanton eye had ever been fixed on you,
no ragged hand had reached out for yours,
and all that was politics, love, booming bells
awaited you again beyond an ocean.
Best thing to do at such times is to imagine
that you can still cry when you've lost your head,
and that the wind will blow lilac blooms
over beds with their torsos and rumpled pillows;
and that on Doomsday
you can stand in a light shirt, light jacket
beyond smoke, taverns, cemeteries,
staring down a country in grand decay,
your head filled with the memory of snow,
snow, snow falling like plaster silently peeling
from a cathedral wall.

(William Jay Smith)

IN FRONT OF SPOTLIGHTS
AND POLICE FISTS

Even the starved seers don't know
what we still have to endure.
Maybe one day no one will be by our side,
only our bags, our hair.
Our unmade beds in the sunlight.
Books will become wise like relics
that were exhumed unharmed.
This unsanctioned epic poem, life,
is written inside them,
the orders of a military review
in blood at Pentecost—
rain's poem,
the poem of man's treachery toward man,
the poem about a world
that perished inside a poem.
But all this is as distant as the beyond,
as if we were watching an ant
at the bottom of a ravine.
It might be summer
or tobacco-yellow fall.
Chestnuts strike the bench.
From the house next door
silver-haired war sobs in a woman's voice.
Suddenly, what is lacking in our lives
begins to throb like some imaginary pain.
Love throbs like a sawed-off right leg.

I'd even submit to interrogation
in front of spotlights
and police fists.

(Nicholas Kolumban)

WITH MY DAILY DEATH

Out of superstition, I'd get drunk for you,
so you won't die.
I'd drink vodka and wine
until I'm sick—
these spirits that poison you like hot peppers.
The Danube would carry my nights and days,
my shadow,
like a rumpled piece of sack.
My torn shirt-sleeve waves on the shrubs
of the river bank,
nudging the gall-yellow roses.
I'd redeem you, love, with my daily death.
I'd search on my knees for a god
that could renew
your darkening cells.

(Nicholas Kolumban)

I BELIEVED THEN

There was nothing I ever wanted more
than that village-outskirts green evening again
—I on my belly in the May grass with you
dress slightly drawn up over your thighs,
and may-beetles flying over us unsuspectingly,
death-doomed guests of the universe;
and I believed then that the world
would take me back again,
earth, trees, illusions surviving the winter,
that the world, tired of its losses, would take me back.

(Kenneth McRobbie and Mária Kőrösy)

POEM, TO MY WELL-WISHERS

You wanted me to lower my voice,
grow a beard, in some warm womanish room-corner
hunt amid the silence for a pin,
a pin it's possible to kill with.
Well, I didn't stay around for your chitter-chatter!
Instead, my body hankered to visit
the cherry-tree hills, their secrets, uncombed roses
where evening comes unexpectedly,
the weeping also comes, and
a half-word, half-smile can be a declaration of war;
but there is always a tomorrow,
snow-dew, wind,
resurrection which as yet I do not know.

(Kenneth McRobbie and Mária Kőrösy)

THE DARK SISTER OF THE AMAZONS

Coming of spring, the bone in my nose sings it and shudders,
great waves of blossom, the bouquets of the flood
soon end up as rubbish,
even the winter sky dissolves like soaked newsprint
unread, and finds its way to the pile.

Snow may still sift now and then at my back,
wild geese from the north circle the nape of my neck,
but my eye which had followed your progress
long through the snowdrifts
would look to the south to find your hair a natural shoreline.

Then we were ill and great sheaths of bandages
wrapped your sliced breast and wrapped me from waist up,
the sword cannot wound so deep in the course of close combat,
nor death's sickle blade cut such a wide swathe
as we could show now to the brightening sky.

Nevertheless, when the sun stands and faces you, strip off
your clothes. Parade your maimed body
before the first green leaf,
every forest was home to us, each patch of grassland,
dark sister of amazons, the wind still remembers us,
it plays round your shoulder, it raises your hair.

(George Szirtes)

TO KEEP WATCH WITH ME

I'm awake. The lake is outside
and the dark of an alien country.
I hear untranslatable bird cries
from under the bushes.
Is somebody being murdered?

My head's heavy with alcohol
and heavy with myself.
Just now in my dream
soldiers ran, naked to their waists,
and combed through the unkempt park
with pitchforks ready to thrust.

Were they looking for me, the old exile?
I can't remember.
Bloodstains darkened a rock.
I saw an overturned barn lantern.
The flame was mixed with mud
and this made everything so finite,
so shameless.

I'd love to sleep out of revenge
to forget my very European nightmare—
the dread of those sprawled on their stomachs.
But I just fumble with things
and putter around.
I turn the faucet on,
let the water run
to keep watch with me
until morning.

(Nicholas Kolumban)

THE WAIT

I'm waiting, I don't know what for.
A train clatters by in front of your house,
soldiers wave out of windows,
their hair whips in the wind then settles
like the flame of a match.
Things go on
when moments ago time stood still:
a cow is chewing its cud,
trees stand around dumbfounded in the summer
like newspaper readers
free from illusion under a wide sky.
They invoke the end of the world.
There will be no blood
   no fire
      no smiles behind the tail that whisks lazily,
     no deluge looking for shelter.
Only breeding flies,
plague-infested shrubs
and the dunghill in the afternoon.

Something has happened,
something that hasn't reached me
but it ought to soar before my eyes
as the words, the starlings,
the moaning waves of the Atlantic swished once
or war's fires,
burning out the eyes of insects.
But now only a whitewashed pigeon flies by,
at an angle,
in front of my face.

(Nicholas Kolumban)

EUROPEAN SUMMER

Light,
   light
      for days now.
Raging summer wherever I go.
The memory of blazing straw-stacks in my eyes,
Rome burning on an infernal fire,
flaming red popes,
   dried sculptured kings.
Europe: a sunflower bending to the ground,
a hornet, yellowly, flies around it,
gothic lace jams on the horizon,
hills of alum closing war
wounds: the remnants of flashing, crystalline
mourning above the undressing towns.
Oven-mouth breathes on me
from the West,
concrete-mouth breathes on me from the East. Lightning
wires burn,
   ornamental hubcaps,
     mirrors,
       heated spokes,
and from the inside, as though platinum-thoughts
embedded in bones burned me:
I'm choking, I'm fleeing
up to the North, to the shady
corners of Finland,
where water, long left to itself,
   sings in water,
     forest stands behind forest,
   the Moon stands behind the Sun
and from behind the Moon
the beasts can hear
my loud heart throb.

(Len Roberts)

STILL LIFE

How could I have known that one day I'd see all those
bits of rubbish again. The still life of beds, chairs,
half-bodies, tousled pillows, but dawn hurled before
me these heaped up ruins of my memories and sins.
   In the light, of course, everything became softer.
In the crooked nook of time there lay upon the tables
at which my lovers had dined: plates, knives, bras,
words chewed to the bone. In the scribbled over margins
of newspapers the sun never failed to set over hips
and buttocks.
   The wings of rotting fire-flies fluttered amongst
the junk like the wrecked doors of crashed cars. And
balls of fluff and dust rolled to and fro across the
places where love-making had consecrated the floor.
   And unexpectedly I had to remember the traditional
end of the world: and thus the love of waters, insects
and continents will pass. Cities will crumble like
rickety rabbit hutches and under iron bridges bloated
carcasses, antlered eiderdowns, will float towards the
sea, but alcohol, smoke and head-splitting nicotine would
have been needed for me to have imagined the galloping
of the Four Horsemen above the garden lettuces.

(Gerard Gorman and Mária Kőrösy)

NARRATIVE AT DAWN

Day is breaking, in red stripes.
This night of mine was the devil's once more.
I dug a deep trench, ankle-deep in water.
From its yellow clay walls
mouldy shreds of cloth hung raggedly out:
shirtsleeves and a coat
and the brimmed hat of a corpse tilted askew.

No, it's not a dream—throbbed the vein above my blindeye:
something happened here, something even I know nothing of,
some futile, delirious sin:
they killed men in a circus act,
there, a broken magic-wand and a gorged-out eye
in the breast-pocket!

Away with the spade,
   the unearthed wand, away with the trench,
and I run: where is the living being to help me
exhume the levelled meadow?
The road,
     the bridge, are empty,
       in the forest vacant swings sway
from the lofty trees,
the sky is sliced from above by an iron-toothed saw,
large blue chunks of sky
thud into the clearings,
smoke and flame dart from where they fall,
but nowhere a man,
nowhere a whining dog,
only discarded tyres like flat, dark jellyfish—
I stop short: this country is no longer my country,
beyond the forest the reedbeds redden,
further still, endless water, thundering nothingness.

(Gerard Gorman and Mária Kőrösy)

SOMEONE COMFORTS ME WITH A POEM

Can you hear it? Someone is reading a poem over the phone:
he comforts me about my loved ones who died,
    about myself
He promises a snowfall on my head
snow on the places we slept—
    on our bed, the forest,
    over the skeletons of yesterday's flowers
and healing quiet in a gentle cellar
where the flames of a plum tree log
flare up
There will be wine on the table
    bread and a red onion
    the light on the sharp knife is the light of afterlife
    and on the timeless, white wall
    an ant, straying away from its troops,
    marches toward a new century
Can you hear it? It's meant for you, too
Don't strike the night with your large, black wings,
    don't strike grief or soot
You're neither an angel nor a condor
You're the sole tenant of a lovely country
Mine even while under your sentence of death
You wear your hair in a bun—
it falls every evening on my wrists
We both turn toward the North Star
Guns may stare at us tomorrow,
    our misled country with its alien, piercing eyes
We won't need your mercy anymore
We lived everything that is called life
    all the worries of the ones who die early
Look: the promised snowflakes flit about already
    and land on our footprints
    that tread on in unison

(Nicholas Kolumban)

EVA KELEMEN'S LAST WILL

When I die, bury me in my winter coat,
in the long one, which covers my ankles.
I'm cold even in the summer grass.
I'm frozen to the roots of my hair.

(*Nicholas Kolumban*)

THE TRACE OF YOUR HAND

My mouth is full of snow,
once more full of snow —
To whom can I tell you've been dead for two hours?
I can only tell myself: the first stranger.
And here a scarf around my neck,
as if I were dressing and going to you,
though I'm just standing beneath a tilted lamp
on the desolate hill,
on my scarf the trace of your hand still.

(Gerard Gorman and Mária Kőrösy)

SHE WANTED TO SAY SOMETHING MORE

She wanted to say something more,
something I should have known of,
perhaps the snow,
perhaps her long hair falling out in clumps,
perhaps the solemn mole-hills of the Mátra,
of which she had so often dreamt,
perhaps the weight of her hand,
perhaps the thought of another war,
perhaps the knives, her veiled wounds;
of the creaking trees below the hospital window,

perhaps the splitting spring which without her
will scatter willow leaves around my face,
perhaps that I should die with her,
perhaps of my muddy shoes in an impassable cemetery.

I watched her mouth, her eyes,
the mistiness throbbing in her body,
the journey of her hand to my hand
but that sentence was no longer there,
nowhere was that word torn by mercy,
just her last smile glowed at me from among the pillows,
her last earthly smile.

(Gerard Gorman and Mária Kőrösy)

THE SUNDAY BEFORE CHRISTMAS

It's the Sunday before Christmas... What shall I buy you?
The sky is open, the shops are open.
        A little more life, if that were possible,
                pine-needle-scented, for Christmas is coming,
and the year's last few sunny days,
                and then the heavy, unrelenting winter rain,
        which would wash me back with you into the earth.
While alive, you made the chestnut foliage here
        bob around my head,
                death was no more—

And, oh, what that terrible change of place did to me!
        You nowhere, and death circling round
                even on the opaque cambers of green Mason jars;
                crawling out of my books
                        like hungry ants from a breadcloth,
        bringing darkness,
    anger, shame,
    crowding nothingness from stairway corners,
    instead of your nightgown, your shroud—

Lord, I have just realized that everyone is mad—
        everyone Death has touched,
    twisting a strand of cold hair around the tongue.
You, even you make me talk to myself
        all along Martyrs Road,
while alkaline melting snow drips on my forehead from the roofs,
        drop after drop, as on one condemned.

(William Jay Smith)

SOMETHING STARTED

Something started,
something entirely new to my life.
It's winter, snow, the roofs are white
and it feels as though my knocking echoes
    through a deserted mill.

I did not run and did not flee anywhere,
yet now my head jolts sideways
like that of a refugee in an uncertain landscape.
Perhaps in a corner of the grey sky
    even corpses lie unkempt.

In the filthy snow I see a shrunken
ring and a mass of swaying black
hair. What else could my ailing
eyes see? From hillside trees
    memories of my body trickle before me.

Now I know: hell was erected piece by piece
like a house, an unscalable towerblock:
glass walls, glass railings, glass stairs
glare at me and I see a transparent bed, too,
    in which I shall lie on my back at night.

Something started,
something entirely new to my life.
It's winter, snow, the roofs are white.
Behind my back smoke and a psalm stumble and from below,
    from the earth, an eternal mouth cries out to me.

(Gerard Gorman and Mária Kőrösy)

FOREST PSALM

I breathe, walk among the trees—
this is now my history.

The forest, an unpublishable manuscript.

The foliage is crossed out
with dark lines by birds.
Branch-explosion,
then silence,
bursting membrane-walls.

*

Rust-spot on moss.

Transitory seasons approach.

The amiable anthill factories
will be plundered by the rains:
the soldiers of autumn manœuvres.

I must learn to be cold once more,
to smuggle the sun and future beneath the earth.

And again life survives through me,
even when shamelessly pushed aside—
my memories will turn the grass green
and the trees sodden once more.

Wherever I step: rocks twinge
in the earth,
like the bony hands of my dead ones,
so that I do not remain alone
and that my body, too, can feel its company.

Thorns continue to fly towards me,
as if trained knives
were swishing.
Patience, patience—I whisper:
in place of a bird's eye a drop of clotting blood.

1973–1981

(Gerard Gorman and Mária Kőrösy)

STRAGGLING NIGHTMARE

I'm sitting in the sunshine,
   getting warm as the rocks
     after a rough, rheumatic winter.
    At my ankle a slight wind stirs in the grass,
your breath from down below, perhaps.

They say I wept months for you.
    That may be; I can't recollect.
     On either side of me nights blackened
   and horses reared with blood-frothed mouths,
as they do when a shell bursts among them.

And trains and cities and a flock
   of crows plummeting headfirst
    and the skidding, burning wrecks after
   midnight on America's roads,
where I waited, mid-dream, for a crash.

I yelled to you: come, there is resurrection
      through my madness, through pain that is
    greater than pain: the severed
  head, the arm, fly toward you
and our eyes meet again—

I'm sitting in the sunshine,
   getting warm as the rocks.
    A winter's straggling nightmare cries out in my bones.
   At my ankle a slight wind stirs in the grass,
your breath from down below, perhaps.

(Len Roberts and László Vértes)

DREAM OF A LAKE

I dreamt of a lake. Can you unravel its meaning?
Its waters were transparent, soft, but lifeless.
Neither fish, nor wild duck, nor dreamy watersnakes
swam there, nor did green veils of weed sway
in the refraction of light above the mud.
The chamber-fluid of gorged out human eyes
can be as cruel and clear,
water and crystal together, eternal, unpolluted.
I went around, as inquisitive strangers
go round war cemeteries,
and looked for a boot, a glove, a tin-spoon,
or at least a filthy lump of stone
to hurl into the gelling water surface,
but only crunching pebbles lay about,
blurred pebbles licked smooth.
I looked at the water. It looked back, a half-hour corpse.
And suddenly I thought of extinct species of birds,
perhaps I'll hear their cries again:
but all I heard was a wailing from inside my ribs,
like tomorrow's murderers bedding down in a haystack.

(Gerard Gorman and Mária Kőrösy)

IT IS TO DIE THAT I KEEP WALKING NEAR YOU

Midnight. The delicate elderberry bushes
    go on growing in the dark
as I walk among them toward your cemetery,
a little drunk and down at heel
    like the poets of old.

In purple novels the Moon moves at such times
    with a diamond violin
and bats sweep down, grazing:
I hear nothing but the whine of a sickly thrush
    under the bushes
    rambling in its dream.

I cry, mourning for you, stop and begin to sing.
    I watch the stars race at break-neck speed,
and must think of you constantly, you
    who became unthinkable
like the afternoon of the world and the wound of the air
    around my mouth.

A word, a whisper, breaks through the dark: you were burning.
    Another: that you are the memory of this dirt road
        down which I stumble blindly
    and that the irredeemable dust
will retain your wanton footprints.

Words, words. The heartbeats of nothingness
    within me: words going to their death
just as I go to my death in the evenings
    near you
down the path of the elderberries, through the heavy dust.

(William Jay Smith)

THE LOOK-OUT TOWER

Up here above the city the wind will not
bring smoke
nor searing noise,
nor the squeak of the tram, nor time either.
The Balkan turtle-dove
with its boat-shaped belly, flies more leisurely
above the look-out tower,
and seeks a parking place
on the disk of the rusted-out, wartime air-raid siren.
Our eyes meet like those of two expelled natives.
It keeps flexing its wings under the soft sky;
I keep flexing my blood-drained memories,
raising them up through the autumn air.

(*William Jay Smith*)

TO POLAND

Poland, Christ-statue struck by lightning,
   around your blackening wounds
      circles the July sunlight,
your bones constantly kissed by flies.

I suffer for you
   as if I too were lying bludgeoned
      in some stinking shed
   gazing at a single carnation
mirrored in watery soup.

I might be your Hungarian refugee, little
   Prince Rákóczi, unsaddled, a student leaning
      on your church walls,
or a soldier just arrived home, bringing with him
   the scent of the woods,
his loved ones dead, buried naked,
while above him the swallows and dazed insects
and the smoke-bonnets of ruined cities swirl
   through the sky—
but what am I to you, pale country of deep faith?
Nobody, just a friend, your nettling Hungarian
haunting your princely streets with the cranberry-
   taste of noon in his mouth,
and who, in his grief,
seeks a lover among your daughters
because, under the spell of the music of your leaves and light,
he wants to touch, to embrace you,
and to endure for hours at the greengrocer's the
   stench of stale beets,
to bear the unbearable,
queuing up for the wildest hope.

July 1981
      (William Jay Smith)

GOOD WE WERE, GOOD AND OBEDIENT

Good we were, good and obedient,
like children hung with cherries in pedestrian precincts,
    we did not tread on the grass, we did not lay mines
    under the beds of dahlias in the park.
Good we were, good and obedient:
when the odd stray dog was kicked or ill-treated
    we winced for him, yes even in our dreams,
    but would avoid the submission in men's eyes,
    as if skirting the pools of blood at an accident.
Good we were, good and obedient,
we saw the cliffs of Georgia in broad daylight,
    and drank its wines,
        we saw the Black Sea meandering home at dusk,
and the old remaining gods without their mouths,
    and dined with delicate stomachs just for the hell of it.
Rumpsteaks with garnish were garnished by Mozart
    from his cold starry podium.
    Good we were, good and obedient,
wind blew and the years dipped below us like cities
    lit up at night and seen from an aeroplane that turns
        very slowly,
    fine flakes of fire, the world's fire, advertisements,
    rose up to meet us,
late for a reception the general burned with his gold epaulettes,
but preferring Jancsó's heavenly women whose bodies
    turned on the screen
of the cinema, and hung their kinky knickers on gravestones,
    we shuddered and shook.
    Good we were, good and obedient,
ill fortune, clad in a skirt, flittered across
        the aching bridge of our noses,
    the past was fully fulfilled with us,

but we were still fondling the memory of war
    as a grand ball with trumpets,
as if in our places a stuffed sack of pink
    lay dreaming in bed, night after night.

(George Szirtes)

THE LONG WINTER'S PSALM

The winter is long, determined never to leave us.
The pigeons of a year are already beaten by it.
They patrol domestic roofs, shuffling and bedraggled,
   like the crippled watchman in the timberyard.

Shrove Tuesday is past, so is Ash Wednesday,
but instead of ashen catkins we have snow again,
although the previous snow
   still lies beneath the gouty bushes.

Old papers and tin cans, beheaded plastic dolls—
my eyes walk among ruins. I imagine my heart
as a repository of such heaps of wreckage.
   I'm full of memories of war, exploded bridges.

Doorhandles, fingers, streets, all are cold to the touch.
Even the traffic between our wary eyes
is reduced to a frozen hulk, a ferry that hoves to and fro
   with a single rook perched on its icy deck.

I still can clearly recall each spring and every summer.
I store a thousand years of chattering birdsong under my pillow,
but I'd have to be quite mad, the village idiot,
   to place my trust in any memory.

God has fallen asleep. Our ancient hopes sleep with him.
The heaters that make saucer eyes at us and imitate
night spirits, merely make us lazy. Beneath the skin
   I must awake new passions in myself.

I hear the refugees of winter shuffling in patrol
down all the centuries; a stifled coughing and cursing.
But something hot arrests me too: their ancient mouths
    protest, their breath is fire between my eyes.

(George Szirtes)

ALL TIME

I long to wall myself in in a windowless
white room, with no other companion beside
my hopes with their conspiracies. All time
would be mine again at last: the winter full of
creaking hayricks, the time of the marching ant,
and the long rains at the end of autumn when scythes
are drenched in the rank grass and bleed like soldiers
wounded at the front. I could be out of date again:
body and soul, nerve and bone stretching out
into infinity. The memory of iron wheels
should not repeat its victory over me, nor of infernal clockwork!
Death should sit on my table like a butterfly fixed
on a pin, and my poem would begin with its immaculate shadow.
I'd write nothing else, my eyes too would write poems
for my staggering nation, and also for you who watch
all that I do with leaden rings round your eyes.

(George Szirtes)

IF YOU BLED

Unconsolable, long week in Finland.
I search for the Sun over the chasing woods,
but only your weak fist could shatter
the rough opaque glass-sky for me.
If you bled, I'd fervently court your dewy wound.

(Gerard Gorman and Győző Ferencz)

ABROAD

I read my friends' thin volumes here abroad.
Their words are overshadowed by the hair of women
hurrying down the street, by rains that clean skyscrapers.
I realize now that they too will grow foreign to me,
that summer will dip like an empty swing above their graves.

(George Szirtes)

CONFESSION TO THE CITY

How much rubbish the wind sweeps down the street,
how many faces drifting, emptied of matter
   and streaks of choking smoke below the city sky!
And how much bleached out love behind the walls!
But when the passions briefly change to green
   as signals do at traffic lights,
the branches which were restrained begin to sway, the rain
   descends from high in towering lacework curtains
 and a brilliant madness shudders
   along the whole length of the tramway,
whistling and whining like a flute
   pitched at high falsetto.

I love you, I love you not...? For thirty years, city,
I have been tearing pages from your calendar.
   I amble down your streets
     with no idea of direction.
Here things lie close to hand and to the body,
closer to delight, to homicide.
The boilers are dragons who open monstrous throats
   to shoot their flames about my face, as in the legend,
and down below, under the crust, your sewers
   throb continuously in eternal squalor.
Am I yours then, city? or simply
   your prisoner?

Often I leave you, deny you and yearn to be where
even now the fire stretches out
  along the earth
   like some exhausted beast of burden,
and in gardens the hedgehogs scuttle, prehistoric representatives
whose velvety mumbling is suddenly rent
   by the squeal of your million windows, your fetters,
your lovely neurotic women who scream out forsaken,

and there I am with them again,
in the lifts full of mirrors, shimmering upward,
   in the hair-raising draughts of the underground,

in multiple reflections from your million eyes and
from my own madness. If you will not accept me,
   only the woods may give thought to my presence, or death
      with his elbows propped on the moon,
and the world won't call on me in an emergency,
won't send for me, won't wait nor pursue me with music,
from which I may learn immortality. You tremble
   excitingly on my white membranes, like
beans on a drum in vibration. Does smoke swallow you up?
Earthquakes perhaps? Burgeoning roses of wildfire? Though I betray you
   I'll perish with you.

                    (George Szirtes)

IT WILL REMAIN A LIVELY MEMORY

Here I am with you,
    and it's good to be with you now.
A butterfly on stone, her wings two burning peacock-eyes
advertises the business of summer,
or perhaps your eyes.

Your body lies beside mine quietly,
    and hums like a radio.
Antennae of grass pick up the signals of your breathing.
Grass-stallions rumble towards you,
and a hundred acres of wheat in green flood down the hill,
but the image of being swept away,
delights us now, as it has always done.

I'll see you again, in little country towns,
    at literary evenings, by lindens with top-knots.
The theatre rings with sounds of weeping, a stream of curses,
but this too you'll escape
before the performance begins
anonymous men beside you form an escort,
and you will follow the wild irrational voices of May.

I feel it already: I should prepare for the pain
    of you *having been*
when you no longer lie by me on lake-shore, in hill-grass,
when in your dreams it is not I who sweeps
the grey and aged ladybirds from your body.

It will be good to gaze upon
    the inviting duel of your lovely breasts:
it will remain a living memory
my pattern of all perishable things.

(George Szirtes)

SLUMBERING ON A TRAIN

The train rocks gently, I close my eyes,
they retain a giddy avenue of trees,
a pond, a puddle, a barren path through fields,
and the pock-marked patron saint of ditches.
And something leaflike too fluttering, green
    between the earth and sky,
though it will never touch ground again.

Each source of irritation slowly dies
and leaves me with the landscape. The chronic
memory of violence dribbles
as white as froth on a dog's rabid mouth.
Click, click,—the wheels run on into infinity
    and take me with them. I leave behind the daily
skirmishes of the body: the tyrannical present.

Is it a waking dream? A rehearsal for a drama
before or after death? Hands float above the summer,
and bellropes swing and droop.
Nothing that touches my temple now has ever
touched it before. She who wept, weeps far away,
    she who undressed for me
under the warm rain, undresses far away.

I hear the rummaging of crickets in distant
withered grass and the dry creaking of a stork's bill.
This would do for me as the last audible sound
would do for a hundred days of dreaming. Click, click—
the wheels run on into infinity,
    and what is to come: plains ever more whiplike,
and ditches ever longer, more extensive.

(George Szirtes)

FAREWELL TO FINLAND

Greyish-blue clouds swim above Finland—
I slide from beneath them, I'm saying goodbye.
Lines from verses clap shut behind me, confused with
raindrops in showers, the crying of the gulls.
What an escort of honour this is in September!
It's easy to reflect: death might have reached me here as elsewhere.
Leaning against the walls of the Rock Temple
I heard the tick-tock of a beating clock
and the ceaseless pulsing of arteries on Orpheus's temple.
I knew I too should never look back again:
let regiments of women walk, blonde and unharassed,
     their limbs bathed in sunlight
     down Mannerheim boulevard;
let them perfume their hands with the early green apples
while they have time.
I'm going in any case, almost on tip-toe,
the cool northern light
sits quietly on my neck like a judgment postponed.
I lose my towns and my cities like this, one after the other,
old navigation routes where boats might find temples of water,
the waters themselves. Though the sea
like a grey veteran of a winter campaign
begins to sing behind me,
its voice hoarse and wild—to me and the limitless sun.

(George Szirtes)

YOU, HUNGRY FOR SUN
*DURING THE FILMING OF PERGŐTŰZ**

What could you have found to say
to those who were dying?
What could you have found to say to those men out there,
stretched on their improvised beds on the battlefield?
In the corner lie dressing,
cotton,
iodine,
bloody medallions
and out in the unweeded garden, spurge
and sandflowers,
tulips from the Don,
and even above the furrowed fields of spring
the bullets fly past on their low trajectories
like swallows hunting for insects.
What could you have found
to say to them there in the waves
that rattled the front,
the stink of mines?
That you are true heroes all, boys drafted in as angels,
that with wounds that blossom like vast scarlet roses
you're healing your country?
That when the women back home come to draw
water at wells, it is your migrant faces they'll see
floating deep at the bottom
and that all the summer will ache after you?
Ache then or burn?
And that great sheaves of straw
will cloud up the sky for your sake?
Or that among long lines of aspens
a chasm will open there on the spot where you laughed?
What could you have said to them there, especially you,
who, conspiring even with mud in its slither and slime

* "Pergőtűz" means "Barrage". It is a documentary film in five parts
dealing with the fate of the Hungarian armies on the Don front
in the Second World War. Csoóri wrote the script.

are continually begging
for life to show pity?
Even now your teeth are crunching at radish,
and you'd like to be gone, to sneak off like some fugitive,
the afternoon tempts you with a lap of flowers.
What could you have found to say to them, you,
you with your hunger for sun, your thirst for eternity.

(*George Szirtes*)

NOVICE NUNS IN ROME

I see the little novice nuns of Rome
   as they float away towards the distant Tiber.
Their dark-blue canvas habits are the bruise
left by a fist under a woman's eye, which pulse and ache
     throughout the early morning.
From the damp lip of the fountain rise
   the lazy butterflies in their slow wake,
from the base of the tower the centuries sigh out.
O Lord O Lord, I mutter my own prayer
   gazing at cracks in the concrete:
what knees, what paradise,
   what breasts anointed with compassion
     are passing purposelessly from the world.

(George Szirtes)

NIGHT JOURNEY THROUGH THE GERMAN FATHERLAND

Darkness and wind. Downstream on the Elbe
a shapeless weight is oozing on the tide.
   A giant sack perhaps,
     perhaps a vessel,
or else some nomadic hill that has lost its way in an earthquake.

The night is cold outside
   the water's cold,
     both are systems of command.

The train sweeps by with all its metal cold.

Withdrawing to the depth of the compartment
   I pass the gaping wounds of Germany
     with eyes downcast.

Do you see me now, hurtling by the river,
   you dead ones with your eyes? You,
bone-citizens, smoke-spirits, can you see me?
Like one who suddenly wakes among the ruins
   after forty years to the high descent
     and scream of burning rafters I should howl
and beat against the window with my fists,
to show that though time passes, the memory
   of every treachery is here
     under my skin,
   all that the war bequeathed to us,
here, here, like a serpent in the arbour.

Small skirts of blood, the poppies of the front,
   church spires shot through the head
     watch me from their low eye levels.
But my hand remains in my lap,
   it cannot respond to them,
my throat will not open for speech,

it's as if someone had stuffed my mouth
    with velvet
        or handfuls of roses.

Inarticulate mounds
    of darkness squat on all the round horizon.
The trees and the columns, the eagles in the stratosphere,
    their terrible aspect,
all melt in the darkness along with my blunt moving shadow.

Downstream on the river
    the shapeless nightmare is still oozing on.
        Perhaps it's a burst sack,
            perhaps a vessel,
or else some nomadic hill that has lost its way in an earthquake.

(George Szirtes)

BLACKBIRD IN THE THAW

It's thawing madly. From the gutter
tender cascades shower down onto the pavement.
A daring blackbird
zig-zags fluttering around them, like reckless kestrels
around Niagara.
Does he play for you? Does this aroused bird
living amongst us, court you?
Or does he provoke the fur-hatted Gods of ageing winter?
Volcanoes weep on the other side of the World, in Mexico:
perhaps, he worries and rages with the colour
of grief on his feathers for them.
We hop with our necks drawn in
towards the spring, under the magical spell of his slush,
ready for grief and pleasure at any hour,
at any minute.

(Gerard Gorman and Győző Ferencz)

PROPHECY

The last spring shall come, the last summer, too,
before their fall, but no judgement, again, shall be passed.
The guilty ones shall sneak shiftily from the rooms,
from beneath the glass chandeliers imitating the sky,
into the open, among the trees
and they shall blend with the rheumatic shadows.
In the parks, crickets,
at the feet of prophesying statues,
retching drunks. No one asks anything.
The faces of the ravaged shall be more harrowed than the criminals'.

(Len Roberts and László Vértes)

HUNGARIAN TITLES

ISBN 963 13 3030 3

Cover photo by László Csigó

Printed in Hungary, 1989
Kossuth Printing House, Budapest